ART OF THE WESTERN WORLD

EARLY CHRISTIAN TO MEDIEVAL PAINTING

CARLO VOLPE

PAUL HAMLYN · LONDON

ART OF THE WESTERN WORLD

General Editor Marco Valsecchi

EARLY CHRISTIAN TO MEDIEVAL PAINTING

Translated from the Italian by Pearl Sanders

Published in the U. S. A. by Golden Press, Inc.,
New York.

The paintings reproduced in this book were photographed by Crea, 2, 8, 9; Giraudon, 7; Istituto Geografico De Agostini, 3, 4, 16, 17; Scala, 1, 5, 6, 10, 11, 12, 13, 14, 15, 18, 19, 20, 21, 22, 23, 24.

Printed in Italy by Istituto Geografico De Agostini S. p. A. Novara 1963

INTRODUCTION

The art of the Middle Ages in Europe developed slowly and uncertainly at first, often seeming to lose its way in the gloomy conditions of catastrophe, despair, cruelty and death, which darkened men's minds in that troubled era. Yet it was to attain remarkable heights of expression, flowering into the ecstatic spirituality of the style we know as the 'Romanesque' and, later, into the beauty and grandeur of the Gothic, with its blend of joyous human feeling and elegant strength. The numerous surviving examples of these styles are among the chief glories of the Western artistic heritage.

Medieval art was, of course, Christian in purpose and inspiration: yet its stylistic origins are to be found in the images of the pagan world. The period from the 4th to the end of the 10th centuries saw the prevalence of a deteriorated late Roman art which was adopted by Christian artists as a means of illustrating the symbols of their faith and the images of their veneration. In the 4th-century mosaics of the Mausoleum of Santa Costanza in Rome, for example, mythological characters (Orpheus, and Cupid and Psyche) are employed to symbolise the teachings of the new religion, and we find similar treatment in the apse mosaics of Santa Pudenziana, also in Rome (the latter have unfortunately been spoilt by restoration).

In the course of the 5th and 6th centuries there evolved, in Syria, Mesopotamia and Alexandria, a somewhat free style of painting which has been called 'neo-Hellenistic'. There are some fine examples of this style in secular art, such as the admirable illuminated manuscript known as the Ambrosian *Iliad*, in Florence. But it was in the spirited and ardent impressionism of Christian artists that this style attained its highest level, as Christian imagery gradually replaced that of the pagan world: a fine example is the Gospel copied by Rabula in a monastery in Mesopotamia in 586, and now in the Laurenziana Library in Florence. In this Gospel, the late Roman iconography was employed in a new form, and from it came one of the earliest portrait types of Christ, which was eventually to take precedence over all others in Western art. This type replaced the delicate beardless versions in early Roman portraits, such as the adolescent, somewhat pagan 'Good Shepherd' in the Lateran church, Rome, the mid-5th-century portrayals in the Mausoleum of Galla Placidia in San Vitale, and the two 6th-century iconographic versions in Sant' Apollinare Nuovo.

In the mosaic decoration of Santa Maria Maggiore, which dates from about 390, and also that of the early 5th-century triumphal arch of Sixtus III, both in Rome, colour was used as a means of attaining vivacity of expression.

Later, in the stylised abstractions of Byzantine art, colour was relegated to a secondary role. Under Eastern influence art took on a more and more abstract symbolism: this symbolism was expressed in the form of a rigid and formal Paradise, such as we find in Ravenna in the Mausoleum of Galla Placidia, or in the Baptistery of the Orthodox, with its frigid ceremonial, or in the awkwardness of the figures in the 6th-century mosaics of Sant' Apollinare Nuovo.

Let us leave Ravenna, the centre of official Byzantinism, and return to Rome for some trace of Early Christian *sermo rusticus et vulgaris*: in the 7th-century church of Santa Maria Antiqua, for example, and in such fragments of catacomb murals as the menacing portrait bust of Christ in the Pontianus catacomb.

On the other hand, in the decorations of SS. Cosma and Damiano and in the Oratory of San Venanzio, by the Lateran Baptistery, rigid adherence to rules and mere technique reduce the fervour of Early Christian inspiration to anodyne litanies. The decline can be seen by making a comparison between these weak decorations and the splendid 4th-century mosaic in the porch of the Lateran Baptistery.

The dedication of the apse mosaic of Sant' Agnese was composed between the years 625 and 638, and the poet evoked in inspired words the miracle of this brilliant if rigid work:

Aurea concisis surgit pictura metallis
Et complexa simul clauditur ipse dies
Fontibus e niveis credas aurora subire
Correptas nubes roribus arva rigans
Vel qualem inter sidera lucem preferet Irim
Purpureusque pavo ipse colore nitens.

(The golden image rises from the fragments,
Gathers and holds close the very light of day,
As at rising dawn from the clear streams
The scattering clouds bedew the fields;
Or as the light among the stars heralds the rainbow
With the gleaming colours of its peacock rays.)

The radiance of this great creative faith was followed by that dark era of iconoclasm which, in the 8th, 9th and 10th centuries, caused virtually every important trace of a living art to be lost. This in spite of the abundance of mosaic decoration in many Roman churches —in Santa Prassede, with its small chapel to St Zeno, and in Santa Maria in Domnica, to name but two; and in spite of the 9th-century frescoes of the crypt of San Clemente (which have certainly been much overpraised). It is to Castelseprio, between Gallarate and Varese, that the admirer of medieval art has to go to find an example of genuine painting: in the little church of Santa Maria foris portas, with its incomparable frescoes depicting stories in the life of the Virgin and a Theophany. These frescoes were painted between the 6th and the beginning of the 10th centuries (one authority has dated them as early 7th century). Here the passion of the miniaturist of Rabula's Gospel embraces a portion of reality where all that matters is the fervour of 'seeing'; this is expressed with an amazement and pathos that were slow to re-appear in Italy (indeed not until the middle years of the 13th century). It is not unreasonable to suppose that the brief outburst of unrestrained freedom in the painter of Castelseprio was the fruit of a rare Italian grafting on to the anti-classical branch of Carolingian art.

But before coming to that ardent spiritual movement revealed by the Carolingian artists to north-western Europe, we should recall earlier events concerning the first appearances of the barbarian Anglo-Saxons, Franks and Visigoths in the Christian world. The earliest and most authoritative models which were then used to illustrate the new moral symbols were always neo-Hellenistic or, more precisely, Byzantine in style. The contact of these peoples with Mediterranean civilisation, which they interpreted very freely, produced some hybrid results. In the art of the miniature, for example, especially in Ireland and England, motifs taken from folklore were intertwined to form complex and colourful geometric patterns. Pre-Carolingian, or more exactly Anglo-Irish, miniatures, were produced during the 6th and 7th centuries in southern Europe as far south as Bobbio and Monte Cassino in Italy, and later in Spain, following the routes taken by the miniaturist monks to the most famous monasteries. The *Book of Kells* in Trinity College, Dublin, the *Bible of Ceolfred* in the Laurenziana Library in Florence, and the *Gospel of St Cuthbert* in the British Museum, all 7th- or 8th-century books, are works of amazing richness and were to inspire Western miniaturists for many more centuries, from Carolingian and Ottonian times until the culmination of the art of the miniature in the Gothic period.

The end of the 8th century saw the birth and growth of that important cultural movement known as the ' Carolingian Renaissance '. In the reigns of Charlemagne and his successors an amazing surge of creativity swept through the arts. This had its greatest effect on the territories of France and Germany, which were most directly subject to that rule, but as manuscript illumination spread, this upsurge was reflected farther afield, in Italy and elsewhere.

Carolingian art first flourished in the atmosphere of Charlemagne's court and was called the art of the ' palatine school ' (after the Cappella di Palazzo, which derives the name *cappella* from its reliquary of the *cappa* or cloak of St Martin). To this school belonged some great scribes and miniaturists, who, with a new pictorial vitality, combined decorative motifs taken from Irish folklore with the courtly themes and brilliant materials of Byzantine art. But this type of decoration, as seen in the *Gospel of Godescalcus* in the Bibliothèque Nationale in Paris, commissioned by Charlemagne and produced between 781 and 783, or in the Soissons *Gospel of St Medard*, of slightly later date (also in the Bibliothèque Nationale), was soon replaced by the more original and profound art of the schools of Tours and Reims, free at last from all classical borrowings. It cannot be denied that occasionally certain classical elements appeared in the works of these artists, but the new art had taken firm root, and if it sometimes had echoes of classical influence then it was from an immeasurable distance. The art of the Carolingians was, in fact, no less inspired than the magnificent Romanesque sculpture of France and Italy of three centuries later. The *Gospel of Ebo* (before 823) and the magnificent paintings of the *Utrecht Psalter*, which seem to be by a Far Eastern artist under the spell of the Apocalypse, made Reims the artistic capital of that period. And later that burning inspiration was fused with the passionate art of Cimabue.

More than five centuries separate the two periods in painting which open and conclude the adventure of the medieval soul, which was to be reborn against the sinister setting of a never-appeased cataclysm, and to wander with the memories of its martyrdom in search of spiritual redemption.

Against that background, after the Carolingians, the miniaturists of the Ottonian era came into prominence. They miraculously produced a renewed artistic culture in the year 1000, at a time when in England in the school of Winchester and later in the school of Canterbury, the message of the *Utrecht Psalter* was to rekindle a fire of enthusiasm. At Treviri and Reichenau, Saxon artists breathed new life into the ancient forms which, when brought into contact with the ardent Christianity of the north, developed into new, hallucinatory images.

The new art of Europe was thus formed by a series of clashes between civilisations, the contrast between new and old providing the vital spark to the artist's genius.

The same process occurred with the two great 13th-century Italian artists on whom the foundation of the Renaissance, first in Italy then in Europe generally, was to be firmly established, with its mixture of sacred and profane. The *Codex Egberti*, in the Treviri Library, already gives vent to the strident pain of Giunta Pisano; and the visionary classicism of the Reichenau miniaturists of the 10th and 11th centuries, between the *Gospel of Otto III* in Monaco and the *Codex of Hitda* at Darmstadt, anticipates with a kind of bewitched frenzy Nicola Pisano's antico-modern cult of the hero.

Italian art in that period of the Middle Ages which saw the birth of Romanesque civilisation, is divided into two great zones of influence. In the northern area, which was dominated or at least deeply affected by the Lombard spirit, affinities with the forms and meanings of Transalpine art developed coherently, following at times a parallel pattern (see, for example, Wiligelmo and the 12th-century sculpture of Emilia and the sculpture of Toulouse in southern France); while in the vast meeting place of the south, highly original forms were generated which yet reflected a substratum of classical Antiquity, as modified by the spirit of Byzantium, if not directly by the Islamic East. In these southern areas, whenever northern European artists appeared—the Norman or Cistercian monks, for example—the greater classicism of the local artists was combined into a new, hybrid, autonomous language of great originality. We see this particularly in the case of architecture, but the rare examples we have in painting (Ferentillo; Sant'Angelo in Formis) are fettered by the influence of Byzantium.

Contact with the forms and images of northern art led to the development of architectural characteristics which were new to Italy. The models were very soon outdistanced in a lively creative evolution which led to such important new elements as the separation of the campanile and baptistery from the central body of the church. In such developments, forms once dear to Early Christian and exarchal classicism were adopted for artistic reasons.

The art of sculpture followed a similar pattern, in which the artists of France, Italy and Spain were united in their use of fantastic images distorted by an excess of vitality into a monstrous world, where men and animals were shown as strange impassioned creatures imprisoned in an unbounded nightmare. In that mixture of belief and fantasy, which was found in the vivid and compelling reliefs which decorated the capitals and which often all but covered the portals, there were no limitations of language; these works spoke the universal language of religious legend and Holy Scripture, mixed with popular fables, in which the erudition of Antiquity was reclothed in a rural and provincial Christianity, in familiar philosophy expressed in sayings and proverbs.

Yet in Italian painting, for example, between the 9th and 12th centuries, there is nothing to testify to that profound wealth of feelings, even at a modest level, if we except the frescoes of San Vincenzo at Galliano. These have the solemn imprint of Ottonian art, while the influence of Byzantine stylisation can still be felt. This Byzantine influence also weakened the inspiration of the fresco painter of Civate.

Economic and political uncertainty greatly afflicted Italy in the 9th and 10th centuries; yet even later there was no stability in art. Artists became wanderers to remote centres, and were to remain so for many years, until they were given security in the 13th and 14th centuries by some well-administered local communities in which self-governing centres of art could flourish. Already, in the 11th to 13th centuries, the new commercial maritime centres of Pisa and Genoa, and in no lesser degree Amalfi and Venice, had proved exceptions to the general state of insecurity. These powerful republics, together with the expanding religious orders (particularly the Benedictines and Cistercians), nurtured the new architecture, and with it, the new sculpture.

Painting, on the other hand, was less fortunate; its creators were either forgetful of the splendour of the past or, as in Palermo or Venice, prone to perpetuate the glittering image of an outdated iconography, in which a rigid and mechanical stylisation transmuted the early fervour of the mosaicists into lifeless patterns. The 12th-century mosaicists of Cefalù and the Palatine Chapel of Palermo, and those who re-commenced the decoration of St Mark's in Venice, were but perpetuators of a remote art—of the imperial power and theological rigidity with which Byzantium re-evoked its lost greatness. Western man had other living symbols and images through which to express his aspirations; and it was the strange fate of painting at this time that it lacked the vitality of sculpture and architecture to render these images. Wall fresco painting, which in the Early Christian period had been lavished on the frozen walls of cemeteries, survives only in the modest little church of Castelseprio. Here the artist, while remembering the neo-Hellenistic miniaturists already foreshadowed the impassioned art of the Carolingians. These surviving works, created in a transient and uncertain era, belonged entirely to a decayed Graeco-Roman civilisation which artists had been adapting to their purpose for centuries.

For that reason it would be pointless to linger at Sant'Angelo in Formis (11th century) or at Ferentillo (12th century) or to try to discern, in the famous frescoes of the 11th-century crypt of San Clemente, traces of the stylised yet vibrant intensity of the 10th-century Ottonian frescoes in St George's church on the island of Reichenau. From these frescoes a straight path leads to the Romanesque sculpture of the following two centuries. But from the Greek mosaics of Sicily and the Balkan frescoes of the Benedictine Renaissance to the stylised mosaics of St Mark's in Venice or the work of Alberto Sotio of Spoleto and Bonaventura Berlinghieri in Lucca, there were transmitted merely a paucity of ideas and an imitation of forms.

It was not until the late 13th century that Giunta Pisano made the heroic effort of breaking the bonds of the Balkan tradition; and this first sign of life passed like a thunderbolt to other innovators of genius. The third Master of Anagni foreshadows Cimabue with almost as profound a spirituality, and presents one of those riddles of art to which there is no solution. So, too, the Master of the Reliquary of Sant'Agata, in Cremona Cathedral, or the Master of San Martino at Pisa; the writings of Longhi shed more light on these events than those of any other writer. In those artists, and in the miniaturist of the Months in Psalter No. 346 at the Bologna University Library, we find the essence of late medieval Italian painting. But that brief period of creative power contained in the strength and the 'historic sadness' of Cimabue was nonetheless to become the living foundation for Giotto's ideal of painting, in which the intellectuality of classical art combined with the life and humanity imparted by these immediate progenitors.

For these reasons, above all, Italian 14th-century painting, named ' Gothic' by the Renaissance, so as to thrust it back within an uncomprehended northern medievalism which was never to break its confines completely, is irreconcilable with the spirit of Transalpine art of the 13th and 14th centuries. This northern art flourished with renewed splendour in the miniature, in stained glass, and above all in panel painting—to the special glory of the school of Paris. But so many artists of sublime genius appeared in Italy during the 14th century that the painting of this period alone would be enough to illustrate many centuries of civilisation; and in its varied tendencies and ideas it brought about (in Italy much earlier than elsewhere) the end of the Middle Ages in Europe.

THE PLATES

Plate 1—Praying Madonna with Child (*middle of the 4th century*). The early Christians wished to decorate their catacombs with paintings, and they began to work out an appropriate symbolism, using Roman and Greek decorative motifs to signify the new meanings. On the roughly plastered walls of the galleries dug out of the tufa, the painters, working by lamplight, traced their images with bold strokes and lines of colour, mainly red on white, following a ' compendiary ' procedure similar to popular painting of the late Roman Empire.

At first they selected very simple subjects, such as cupids, or vine tendrils, with which they decorated the vaults and recesses of the crypts, as in pagan art; these paintings, by their symmetrical composition, clearly revealed the influence of classical models. Within these geometric compositions were later placed the most varied decorative elements, suggested and justified by the symbolic meanings imposed by Christian artists. Great use was made of figures of animals, such as the fish, the lamb, the drinking stag, the peacock, the dove—the symbolism of which was obvious and familiar to all the faithful. From pagan myths, characters such as Orpheus and Psyche were taken, transposed to illustrate Christ preaching and the life beyond the grave. One of the most widely diffused images was that of the Good Shepherd with the Lamb on His shoulders, derived from the classical Hermes bearing the young Dionysus.

The Old Testament figures in other catacomb paintings, at first infrequently, but becoming more frequent with the diffusion of holy texts and the parallel growth of a symbolism which interpreted all the Old Testament stories as prefigurations of the Gospels or as allusions to doctrines inherent in the faith, such as the salvation of the soul, or the doctrine of Divine Mercy. Among these symbolic representations we find: Daniel in the Lions' Den; the life of Moses; Jonah and the Whale; the Sacrifice of Isaac; Noah's Ark.

Knowledge of the Gospels spread during the latter part of the 2nd century, and from them were drawn episodes from the life of Christ, but completely omitting the drama of the Passion. The stories illustrated were the Adoration of the Magi, the Baptism of Jesus, the Resurrection of Lazarus and the Healing of the Paralytic; the simple image of the Madonna and Child was frequently seen as early as the 2nd century. One of the earliest exam-

Plate 1. *Praying Madonna with Child.*
Middle of the 4th century. Rome, Ostrian catacomb.

Plate 2. *5th-century Icon.*
Rome, Santa Maria Nova.

ples of this image, which was destined to become universal, is the fragment of a fresco in the catacomb of Priscilla, where beside the seated Madonna holding the naked Child on her lap we see the prophet Isaiah announcing the coming of the Messiah. The unusual spontaneity of the gestures places this fragment among the most significant of catacomb paintings. Another interesting picture of the Madonna and Child is the 4th-century fresco in the Ostrian catacomb. The Virgin faces the beholder with hands raised in an attitude of prayer. The two figures are stiff with solemn dignity. Gone is the simple candour of the fresco in the catacomb of Priscilla, with its ingenuous and kindly message; the Ostrian fresco is aligned to the contemporary art of the Christian Orient, in which the once severe portraits of the Fayum have now assumed the fixity of an idol.

But the most frequently recurring image of all in the frescoes of the catacombs is that of the 'Orans', a female figure praying with raised arms, in the Oriental manner; this figure, as well as continually reaffirming the need for prayer, seems also to symbolise the beatitude of the soul. The best known of these, and deservedly, is the Orans of the catacomb of St Calixtus, drawn with only a few strokes of colour, in the best 'compendiary' tradition which, as in several similar cases, is redeemed from the banality of certain hurried, late Hellenistic productions.

Plate 2—5th-century Icon. The icon of the Madonna and Child now in Santa Maria Nova is supposed to have been brought to Rome from the city of Troia by Angelo Frangipane. The icon was almost certainly in the church of Santa Maria Antiqua at the foot of the Palatine; and we are told that Pope Sergius I (678-701) had a silver coating put over it which left only the faces uncovered. In the 13th century the icon escaped the fire in the basilica which occurred under Honorius III. Recently restored to its original state, it was believed to be 13th century, but the removal of successive layers during its restoration revealed its 5th-century origin.

The story of how this icon was restored is most exciting. An inscription reading: *Petrus Tedeschi restauravit 1805*, was found on the back, and when the 19th-century overpainting had been half removed, there was revealed a poor 16th-century painting by a follower of Antoniazzo Romano, which clumsily covered not only the heads but the whole figure of the Child and the head and shoulders of the Madonna. But underneath that layer there came to light an early 13th-century painting of which only the heads could be seen. This had already been classified as belonging to the school of Rome of the 13th century; whereas the two faces brought to light are typical of the Tuscan School of the early 13th century, with stylistic affinities to the Berlinghieri of Lucca.

But the story does not end here. The removal of the 13th-century layer finally revealed the original icon, which was painted with wax on two fragments of canvas stuck on to the panel. It was established that as the warp and the woof of the two fragments of canvas were not parallel, the fragments must have been cut down from a larger painting which was originally all on canvas (we have early records of paintings in wax or encaustic) and stuck on wood to prevent their tearing. Only these two fragments could have been seen through the apertures in the silver coating ordered by Sergius I. In the 13th century the two heads were completely repainted in egg tempera, as they had become darkened by smoke and dust. The 16th-century completion of the figures must have occurred when the silver coating was removed, we do not know for what reason. This then is the history of the early icon, which, larger than its present size, probably represented the Madonna enthroned, holding the Child, who gives His benediction, on her lap, against a blue background, as can be glimpsed from an original fragment.

This inquiry into the history of the painting cannot fail to be of interest, as this is almost a unique case and of such an early date. In preparing the flesh colours, the artist retained the distinction between the sexes, which had been vital to classical painting. The Madonna's face, on a base of green wax, upon which are painted successive shades of clear tones, has the diaphanous and bloodless appearance which is to be found for many centuries to come, even as far as Duccio; the flesh of the Son, on the other hand, is painted in yellow, brown and pink shades superimposed on a preparation of reddish wax. This method of preparing the colours would in itself suffice to prove the very early origin of the icon; but this is also emphasised by the characteristics of style—the well-defined and carved-out volumes, the classical Greek nose, the large, humid astonished eyes—which clearly place this work as a masterpiece of the late Roman Empire influenced by Hellenistic traditions.

This work is dated as of the first quarter of the 5th century. As the paintings which have come down to us from that early age are so few, apart from some catacomb frescoes, mosaics, stained glass, or very rare panels such as the Fayum portraits, the importance of this find can be well appreciated, particularly as this icon is a work of the highest artistic merit, representing the greatest cultural achievement of that age.

Plate 3—Moses Removing his Sandals before the Burning Bush. (*Mosaic*). The church of San Vitale, begun by Bishop Ecclesius after the death of Theodoric, was consecrated by Bishop Maximianus in 547. The presbytery and the apse, which are decorated with brilliant mosaics, are the most precious parts of this noble edifice. In the vault of the apse, the Redeemer, seated on a globe, is flanked by two Archangels, by St Vitalis and by Bishop Ecclesius. Low down, on the sides of the apse, are placed the processions of Justinian and Theodora bringing gifts to the church. The presbytery is decorated with leaf patterns on the vault, circular medallions of the Apostles in the intrados of the ingress arch, the Evangelists at the sides of the triforium, and stories of Moses and Abraham in lunettes and on the walls.

The presbytery mosaics differ considerably from those in the apse; there is a decided unity in the inspiration, and the work appears to spring from one mind; the themes are closely linked to form a cycle relating to the faith and the celebration of the Mass. These mosaics show an unusual liveliness of narration which sets them apart from the interpretations of Oriental Byzantinism.

The extreme simplification of this narrative rhythm is not, however, without echoes of the classical tradition, which was very much alive in the mosaics of the Mausoleum of Galla Placidia and far from extinguished in Ravenna, even in the 6th century. In the biblical series the artists are still aware of the values of structure and weight, which the bright colour in no way minimises.

The mosaic showing Moses on Mount Horeb unloosing his sandals before the burning bush is among the most significant of the series. In both this mosaic and the adjoining one, showing Moses feeding the flock, the sparkling whites of the clothes stand out brilliantly against the delicate green which is the background to all these biblical stories.

The whole range of the presbytery mosaics is intended to exalt the doctrine of the Gospels

Plate 4. *Justinian and his Retinue.*
Mosaic. Ravenna, San Vitale.

Plate 3. *Moses Removing his Sandals before the Burning Bush.*
Mosaic. Ravenna, San Vitale.

and to symbolise the celebration of the Mass. In the arch leading into the presbytery are circular medallions with busts of the Apostles and Christ, and on the vault four angels are shown lifting up the Lamb. The Evangelists are depicted on the side walls, and facing them are the prophets Jeremiah and Isaiah, together with episodes from the life of Moses. In the *Offering of Abel and Melchizedek*, the *Hospitality of Abraham*, and the *Sacrifice of Isaac*, the sacrifice of the altar is foreshadowed. The decoration of the vault is of particular interest: the entwined garland and acanthus scroll forming a rich lattice-work is a splendid adaptation of a favourite Hellenistic theme.

The mosaics in the presbytery are connected with the apse mosaic showing Christ (depicted in the Western manner, without a beard) seated in majesty with Bishop Ecclesius presenting a model of the temple. The presbytery mosaics are easier to date than those of the apse, where laws of space and time are abolished in a splendid abstract symbolism.

Plate 4—Justinian and his Retinue. On the sides of the apse of San Vitale are two large mosaics of the Emperor Justinian and the Empress Theodora with their retinues. Since Archbishop Maximianus, elected in 546, appears in one of the mosaics, and in the other Theodora, who died in 548, is shown as still being alive, it is possible to give a fairly precise date to these two mosaics as about fifteen years later than the presbytery decoration and a little less than fifteen years after that of the shell of the apse. The mosaics of Justinian and Theodora, besides serving as reminders that the basilica did not lack imperial donors, represent the ideal participation of the donors in the consecration of the basilica. There seems to be a slight movement towards the end of the apse.

The Emperor, described by Procopius of Cesarea as an obese man of medium height, is depicted here as tall and lively; the portrait of Archbishop Maximianus seems to have borne a closer resemblance to the original; with sharp and decided features in a lean face he seems the best defined of all the characters, and as it was he who commissioned the mosaic he must also have been present when the work was in progress.

Some have thought to recognise in the ecclesiastic between the Emperor and the Archbishop that Julianus Argentarius who was *praepositus fabricae*; but this identification remains uncertain, as does that which would name the ecclesiastic holding the Gospel next to Maximianus as his successor Agnellus. It is still more difficult to accept the first of Justinian's retinue as Belisarius.

In these groups of figures, as in the mosaic of Theodora's procession, the artist has endeavoured to individualise the characters without lessening the static and hieratic quality of the composition. To this end he has modelled the figures with great precision, and has concentrated entirely on effects of colour. It is for this reason that these two mosaics are quite distinct from all other mosaics in Ravenna, and even in the presbytery of San Vitale itself. In the Justinian mosaic, the figures stand against an abstract background in a golden light which thrusts the elongated figures forward. The whites of the sacerdotal garments and the military cloaks are of extraordinary brilliance beside the imperial purple; but it is perhaps in the mosaic depicting Theodora and her retinue that we find the greatest chromatic splendour.

Plate 5—Frescoes of the Lower Church. San Clemente, Rome. (*9th century*). In the lower church of San Clemente, in Rome, scenes

Plate 5. *Ascension*.
9th century. Rome, San Clemente.

of the life of Christ were painted, of which only a few remain: the *Marriage at Cana*, the *Crucifixion*, the *Marys at the Tomb*, the *Descent into Limbo*, and the central *Ascension* on the wall of the entrance. The date of this cycle can be fixed owing to the figure of Pope Leo (847-855) who appears at one side of the Ascension fresco with a squared nimbus to signify that he was alive at the time the fresco was painted.

This Ascension is undoubtedly the most important of the frescoes, and to it the unknown painter devoted the greatest care. Christ appears within a mandorla, supported by four angels, against a starry sky. Below, the Virgin is shown in prayer, while the Apostles on both sides participate with great solemnity.

The keynote of this phase of the decoration of the lower church of San Clemente is an exceptional vivacity for that time, attained by means of a bold outline and the very imaginative use of colour (behind the Apostles, for example, there are vivid strokes of red and yellow).

But the church of San Clemente is better known for its series of early 12th-century frescoes, depicting three episodes from the legend of St Clement, one of St Alexis and other minor scenes. It is by a study of these frescoes that we are able to understand the significance of the Roman school, which, because of its classical tradition, managed to isolate itself from the Byzantinism latent in all contemporary Italian painting. To this category belong also the paintings of San Bastianello, on the Palatine, and of Sant' Urbano alla Caffarella, near the catacomb of Praetextatus on the Via Appia, which are dated 1011. The ornamentation in San Clemente shows a marked classical influence; but the painting of the figures themselves shows that the artists had recourse to modes and conventions of art going back several hundred years. Effects of depth and sharp modelling are renounced for a stylisation of figures in improbable surroundings of vaguely classical architecture. Also taken from classical painting is the use of pale backgrounds, against which the stories are enacted. Reds, ochres and whites are the predominant tones, and the figures stand out sharply. These figures are joined in a slow rhythm where the distinction between refinement and conventionality may appear elusive. These very detailed and decorative ' stories ' relate without convincing, with refinement but without real feeling, in contrast to the miraculous Castelseprio, which with far greater conviction brought about the strange revival of all that was best in Hellenistic civilisation.

Plate 6—The Archangel Raphael. (*Last third of the 11th century*). In the main apse of the church of Sant'Angelo in Formis, Abbot Desiderius (1057-87) is shown presenting the model of the church. It is thus possible to give a fairly precise date to the frescoes, whose dependence on the church of Monte Cassino is also shown by this fresco. But with the destruction of the superb church of Monte Cassino, decorated with mosaics by artists who had gone there specially from Constantinople, it is more difficult to place this Benedictine painting, the unique survival of the many which once decorated the churches of southern Italy.

The decoration consists of the *Last Judgment* on the inner façade, Old and New Testament stories in the aisles, and the *Benediction of Christ*, in the large apse, which contains in a lower fillet images of the three Archangels, St Benedict and Abbot Desiderius; on the right apse are the *Madonna and Child*, and a fillet with figures of saints.

It is not easy to say if these frescoes were influenced in any way by those of Byzantine decoration in the abbey of Monte Cassino. However, the presence of Byzantine artists at Sant'Angelo in Formis is shown by the paintings in two lunettes over the church portal of the Archangel Michael and the Virgin, which are certainly earlier than any of the frescoes just mentioned.

Byzantine elements were adopted by the artists who painted the apse frescoes, although nuances of light and shade gave way to bold colour contrasts. These elements can be found too in the iconography and in the portrait types and their attitudes. The combination of these elements with a rich and varied palette constitutes the originality of this style, which is particular perhaps to the artists of the Campania. In the figures of the two Archangels, in particular, 'the clothes, the head-dresses, the attitudes, the application of the colours, the conventional breaking up of light, the general impression, follow the Byzantine pattern; but the violent contrasts of colours —although not unknown in Byzantine art, in the now hidden mosaics of the cupola of Salerno Cathedral for example—are out of keeping with the style of the period. Red hair against a yellow nimbus, white face with livid shadows, the cheeks speckled with red crescents, and the figure rising with its multi-coloured wings against the deep blue background; yet all with no more relief than was allowed by the Byzantine formula' (Toesca). The adaptation by the painter of Sant'Angelo in Formis of Byzantine models to his own style should thus be understood not as a return to Ottonian methods but as a provincial interpretation of Byzantine detail.

It is impossible today to find any decoration to compare with that of Sant'Angelo in Formis; not in the Campania, where the fresco cycles of that period have been lost, nor elsewhere, since the most important centres in all Latium, including Rome, present quite different characteristics.

Plate 7—Saints Cyprian and Sabinus Before Maximus. (*Early 12th century*). The frescoes of Saint-Savin-sur-Gartempe are among the most important series of Romanesque frescoes in European painting. They cover the whole vault of the nave, the crypt, the atrium and the gallery. The vault decoration consists of a series of Old Testament stories, together with figures of prophets: the six stages of the Creation, events in the life of Adam and Eve and their children, as far as the Curse of Cain, and the Ascension of Enoch; stories of Noah, Abraham, Joseph and Moses.

It is interesting to see how the symmetrical arrangement of these stories follows the plan of the creators of *broderies* of the Bayeux type. In the same way, in the vault decoration of Saint-Savin the stories are arranged in a continuous frieze, together with mythological subjects and leaf patterns which form an unusual counterpoint to the main narrative. This is the more exceptional in that we know of no similar juxtaposition of sacred and profane in other pictorial cycles. All the frescoes in Saint-Savin follow a strict chronological sequence, yet the quality varies considerably, especially as one passes from the church to the crypt.

The crypt frescoes are earlier and more modest in tone, unlike the elegant and almost startling stylisations in the church. They illustrate episodes in the lives of St Sabinus and St Cyprian, culminating in their martyrdom. Although partly damaged by damp and candle smoke, these frescoes are the best preserved, as they were not harmed as the church frescoes were by exposure to light. The colours are sharp and intense and the effect of the frescoes is powerful although there is some evidence of hasty execution.

It is highly probable that, as in the apse fresco of the *Benediction of Christ* in which Christ is surrounded by symbols of the Evan-

SSA DEDRVNT · SVBIVGA QVEM X
R
F

gelists, in which we see the presence of an iconographic model, so also in these stories of St Sabinus and St Cyprian the artist may have taken as a model some earlier miniature. The figures show the inertia of a copy and lack the freshness which gives such intensity to the frescoes in the nave.

Several painters worked on the frescoes of Saint-Savin, but their homogeneity indicates that they were from the same workshop. Besides the stylistic points they have in common, which are easily grasped by the expert eye, the same rule governs the proportions: the figures are more slender in proportion as they recede, which explains why the figures of the crypt and the atrium have less impact than the supple figures of the nave. The artists already had a feeling for the monumental, which they achieved by vigorous colour contrasts, decided outlines and simplified compositions.

These artists are inspired by Carolingian art as reflected in 9th-century miniatures, perhaps with later Anglo-Saxon modifications. This cultural heritage appears again in other pictorial cycles of south-western France and the Loire valley. Centres like Brinay and Tavant show this common Carolingian background, in contrast to those which still kept faith with the ancient formulas of Byzantium. Saint-Savin, however. remains one of the culminating points of Romanesque art, both for its monumental organisation and its completeness.

Plate 8—Detail of the Apse Frescoes. San Clemente, Tahull. From Tahull, a modest village in the Pyrenees, come some of the most interesting Romanesque paintings in all Spain. In 1123 two churches were consecrated there, which were in themselves two important monuments of 12th-century architecture. These were the churches of San Clemente and Santa Maria. In San Clemente an artist commonly known as the Master of Tahull worked, whose paintings are believed to have been of the same date as the consecration of the church. The unknown painted in the apse the majestic Pantocrator among the Evangelists, and below it the saints were represented in a frieze, not, as was customary, in a heavenly arch.

In grandiose dimensions, the ancient Byzantine theme is endowed with majesty, to which conciseness of composition and the piling on of dark colours contribute no small part. The drawing is most vigorous, the salient points being strongly emphasised, and the mood is completely free from the grim and sombre melancholy of the Pantocrators of Sicilian mosaics. Here the boldness of the style produces most unexpected effects, culminating in amazing inventions of pure humour in the representations of the symbols of the Evangelists, or in the story of the beggar Lazarus at the well-fortified door of the rich Epulon, or again in the painting of the hand of God, which appears to give blessing out of infinite space, through an optical illusion. These episodes reveal a candid and profound religious feeling, expressed in a majestic and stark language, the ideal instrument by which to pass on the message of the faith to the worshippers.

These paintings are influenced by Moorish art, which spread in the 10th and 11th centuries, at the time when the decisive characteristics of the art of the whole Romanesque era in Spain were fixed. The lack of interest in relations of volume, certain bold stylistic effects, and in general the portrait types, clearly indicate Moorish influences, now transmuted into the new Romanesque spirit in which abstraction is superseded by the eloquence of gestures and passions. What had been symbolic and ritualistic now becomes a day-to-day eloquence, and the Pantocrator persuades without overawing.

Plate 6. *The Archangel Raphael.*
Last third of the 11th century. Capua, Sant'Angelo in Formis.

Plate 7. *Saints Cyprian and Sabinus before Maximus.*
Early 12th century. Saint-Savin, Crypt of the Abbey Church.

Plate 8. *Detail of the Apse Frescoes.*
San Clemente at Tahull. Barcelona, Museum of Catalan Art.

It is probable that after his work in this church the same artist went on to the Cathedral of Roda de Isabena in the province of Huesca, where we find a few traces of frescoes; we find in many churches in Aragon, also, signs of this artist's authority over those who worked there. It is possible as well to trace these connections through history, when we remember that the church of San Clemente of Tahull was consecrated by Ramon de Roda, who was almoner to the King of Aragon, and that the village of Tahull was dependent on the Count of Pallars-Jussa, a member of the Aragonese court.

The decoration of the lateral walls of San Clemente was the work of another painter, best known for the *Last Judgment,* painted in the church of Santa Maria and now in the Barcelona Museum. His extremely simple and vital work points to his Catalan origin and distinguishes him from the Master of Tahull because of his more subdued colouring and lesser power of invention.

Another artist painted in the church of Santa Maria, perhaps from the school of the Master of Tahull, but his work is less inspired. To him are attributed the frescoes at Maderuelo in the province of Segovia, and at Berlanga in the province of Soria, which would appear to form a homogeneous group with those of the two Tahull churches, if one bears in mind that such homogeneity does not always imply that all the work was by one hand.

Plate 9—Visitation. Frontal of Mosoll; (*Early 12th century*). Romanesque panel paintings were to be found in Catalonia in particular; originally details of larger works, they finally acquired recognition as works of art in their own right. Placed above the altar, they functioned as a 'sky' to the ciborium, and as such usually represented Christ in Majesty and the symbols of the Evangelists; more often they started as altar-pieces (set in front of the altar in place of the richly worked metal altar-pieces frequently to be found in the early Middle Ages).

Often the panels were painted by the same artists who painted the frescoes in the church, as we can see by comparing the frescoes of Seo de Urgel with the panels from the same church, now in the Museum of Catalan Art in Barcelona. Sometimes the same themes are used in both, for example episodes of the life of the patron saint of the church. It may also happen that the figure of the saint is given a prominent position in these panels, in place of Christ or the Virgin in Majesty. But this occurs later on, when the panels themselves become smaller and have the function of describing and narrating facts (especially those concerning the life of the saint) rather than teaching by means of symbols.

Later, towards the end of the 13th century, the central figure tends to disappear, because the panel is subdivided into equal parts and is then usually transferred from the lower to the upper part of the altar, acting as a true retable. Although specifically religious in intent, as time went by these panels became more discursive and naturalistic and gradually took the place of mural decoration. Their reduced size made them more marketable; and the commissions of rich and powerful donors, including mercantile corporations and civil communities, led to a more everyday interpretation of religion. To the local trends were brought first French influences, then Italian, in a fruitful circulation of culture.

The centre of the greatest activity in panel painting in Spain was Urgel, in the Pyrenees. From Urgel came the artist who painted the important frontals of Hix and Urgel. We find the strength and authority of the large fresco paintings of the apse of San Clemente

Plate 9. VISITATION
(Frontal of Mosoll; early 12th century) Barcelona, Museum of Catalan Art.

at Tahull in these small-scale works which some scholars believe to be the work of the same artist.

Another very likely pairing is that between the frontal of Espinelvas in the Vich Museum and the frescoes of Santa Maria at Tarrassa, depicting *Christ in Majesty* and the *Martyrdom of the Archbishop of Canterbury*. Yet another group of works is by a painter known as the Master of Llussanés, which includes the frontal of the *Life of the Virgin*, also in the Vich Museum, and the frescoes on the tomb of St Paul of Casserras.

This panel painting, which we find in Catalonia in such close relationship with great mural decoration, has no parallel in other western regions of Spain, where it does not appear until the end of the 13th century.

Plate 10—Descent into Limbo. (*Mosaic*). The first mosaics in St Mark's in Venice were begun by artists of the school of Torcello at the time of the second restoration of the basilica, in 1071, following the Byzantine tradition of Ravenna. Only very few of the original mosaics can now be seen: Saints Peter, Mark, Hermagoras and Nicholas in the apse, and the Apostles in the niches of the portal. These figures must have been executed between 1071 and 1112 by artists from Torcello. But the original decoration was much fuller and more complex, following a plan believed to have been evolved by Abbot Joachim da Fiore. If today we can no longer grasp the original plan, that is because of the many interruptions to which the work was subject and especially the many retouchings which extended and changed it. One part of the mosaics, as in Ravenna, was dedicated to the exaltation of the church itself, in which a series of Roman origin is associated with the traditional and ritualistic theology of Byzantine art. This Byzantine cycle is developed in the two arches depicting the *Apocalypse* and the *Paradise*, and in the three cupolas of the atrium: the cupolas depicting *Emmanuel*, the *Ascension* and the *Pentecost*. The mosaics of the two cupolas of the transept only in part develop Christological themes, which are fully treated in the area below the Ascension cupola. To the sides, on the walls and between the columns, is depicted the glorification of St Mark and of the saints who are connected with the religious life of the Venetian lagoon.

Great destruction was caused by the fire of 1106, and about the middle of the 12th century the work of restoring the *Emmanuel* and *Pentecost* cupolas was begun. In contrast to the original decoration, which was greatly influenced by the monastic current of Byzantine art, the new mosaics were primarily linear, with the consequent breaking up of the light, and in them the neutral gold background contrasted with the decisive drawing and significant movement of the figures. These are the characteristics of the mosaics which belong to this phase of the reconstruction, which lasted until the early 13th century when the mosaics of the *Ascension* cupola were restored and stories from the life of the Virgin, the Apostles and Christ were added under the arches and on the walls below. In these mosaics in particular the courtly Byzantine tradition of Daphni was debased by the influence not of Western Romanesque, as the artists intended, but of hackneyed formulas from Eastern art, which had no lack of such gloomy and obscure works.

In the series of episodes from the life of Christ, Toesca has grouped as the works of a single artist the *Entry into Jerusalem*, the *Washing of the Feet*, the *Last Supper* and the *Feeding of the Multitude.* The central cupola depicting the Ascension is the work of a different artist and is more abstract in character. Also by this artist are the stories from the Passion, below the cupola. There the *Descent into Limbo*, when compared with that at Daphni, appears so overcharged as to be grotesque, all its effect being obtained by the crowding of the composition which culminates in the image of Christ. A similar but less pronounced tendency is to be seen in the mosaics of St Paul's in Rome, which date from about 1218, and were the work of artists brought there specially from Venice. The comparison enables us to date the mosaics of St Mark's as a little earlier than this.

Plate 11—Episodes in the Life of St John. (*Fresco*). The frescoes in the crypt of Anagni Cathedral are believed to have been painted between 1231, when the mosaic floor was laid, and 1255, the year of the reconsecration of the church. The artists who shared in this work kept to a single and coherent iconographic plan whose complexity cannot but surprise us: from the Creation to the stories of the Holy Ark and then to the legends of the saints who were the protectors of Anagni. The themes chosen in the frescoes relate to the solemn consecration of the crypt and to the rite of the deposition of important relics. The author of the iconographic plan aimed, with extraordinary breadth of vision, at a synthesis of the composition of the universe, microcosmic man and his moral and physical equilibrium—indispensable data for those who frequented those holy places. Still in connection with the service of dedication were chosen the characters in the scenes: Abraham, Melchizedek, Elijah, Saul and Samuel; there were also theophanies from the Apocalypse and scenes from the lives of the saints, as well as effigies of these saints.

These figures are very richly ornamented, in a return to the tradition of a kind of medieval Roman classicism; well-known imitations of ancient grotesque works are found both at San Clemente and Castel Sant'Elia near Nepi. The arrangement of the frescoes is explained in the same way, with the scenes following each other inside the vaults and around a central ornament.

The first of the artists of Anagni, who was akin to the painter of San Silvestro at Tivoli, took from Roman tradition a part of the iconographic material, although not the boldness of outline and the intense colours. This artist therefore stands apart from the painters of the Roman school, with their frequent use of Byzantine forms which they expressed clumsily.

A second artist painted the *Episodes in the Life of St John,* a detail of which is shown here. This artist seems to have taken as model the most sterile phase of late Byzantine art. An example of this exists in the mosaics of St Paul's Outside the Walls, in Rome: '... ashen and expressionless faces, lifeless folds, harsh contrasts of light, conventional drawing' (Toesca). These are the characteristics of the mosaics, which in many respects resemble the contemporary Legend of San Silvestro in the Church of SS. Quattro Coronati.

But if Anagni merits a very high place in the history of Italian Romanesque, it is owing to a third unknown artist, to whom are ascribed the *Legends of San Silvestro.* 'His sparkling manner, his bold "impressionism", his sense of pathos (he is the only artist, before Cimabue, to be moved by the figure of St Francis), are close forerunners of the great Pisan Master of the Madonna of San Martino' (Longhi). The very different style of this third painter of Anagni reaches out to the growing Romanesque ferment in Tuscany, and is far above the sad and lifeless late medieval neo-Hellenism. To appreciate fully the contribution of this true painter, says Longhi,

Plate 11. *Episodes in the Life of St John.*
Fresco. Anagni Cathedral.

Plate 10. *Descent into Limbo.*
Mosaic. St Mark's, Venice.

we must consider how we can 'enlarge and colour our picture of the decades in which Giotto was formed so as to arrive at an understanding of why the same language was used by the greatest artist of the crypt of Anagni, the Master of the Madonna of San Martino and Cimabue, and why it is on these artists almost exclusively that our attention must be focused in the study of the highest creative values of our 13th century, as far as central Italy is concerned.'

Plate 12—CIMABUE: Crucifix. The Crucifix in the church of San Domenico at Arezzo was ascribed to Cimabue by Pietro Toesca, and scholars all concurred in this attribution which enables us to see the early course of this artist, who was the greatest of all in the decade 1260-70. The gravity and severity of his inspiration lend an awesome expressiveness to the art of this great initiator, whom Vasari called the father of 'painting in an everyday language', in other words, the father of Italian painting. 'So one sees that the Greek manner, first with Cimabue, then with the help of Giotto, died out entirely, and from it a new art was born,' and '... it was Cimabue who was almost the main cause of the renewal of the art of painting.' The Arezzo Crucifix here reproduced represents the re-awakening of the 13th century to the expressive world of painting. The formula of Christ tortured by pain, which became the symbol for all religious meditation, came from the sharp, almost fierce, spiritual language of the Pisan Giunta. But Cimabue gave it the mortal weight of a greater physical illusion, so opening up areas which Italian painting had not yet realised fully, and at last rendered painting worthy of taking its place beside Romanesque sculpture and the Carolingian and Ottonian miniature.

It was as if paying a debt to history that Cimabue gathered up and re-animated the sad splendour of the earliest neo-Hellenistic painting; but he also borrowed from Carolingian art, for long suffocated in Italy. Cimabue's return to the living sources of the Latin world, beyond the rigid art of the Balkan painters, was primarily a recovery of faith in the souces of life and expression, and was part of the Italian rebirth in all the arts which took place in the 13th century.

Like the third painter of Anagni, but with a larger body of work than was allowed to that artist, Cimabue eloquently expresses Longhi's 'Ancient and Ruinous Italy' of the Middle Ages. He spoke to Christian artists in the voice of Jacopone da Todi, and gave to worldly things the harsh bitterness of the marbles of Nicola Pisano.

Cimabue's influence grew rapidly in Pisa and Rome between 1270 and 1280. In Rome, which was again enjoying a brief period of vitality and splendour, a document of 1272 mentions 'Giovanni, or Cenni di Pepe, called Cimabue', and it is possible that a meeting took place there between the Florentine artist and the unknown painter of Anagni. But Cimabue's work in Pisa was obviously influenced by the Pisan school of sculpture: for example, the *Maestà*, now in the Louvre, which was formerly over the altar of San Francesco in Pisa. As Salmi and Toesca have pointed out, it was at that time perhaps that Cimabue collaborated in the mosaic decoration of the Florence Baptistery, which, owing to similarities with the work of Nicola Pisano, may be of an even earlier date than 1271, which is the earliest date given for those famous mosaics.

But Cimabue's greatest works are the Crucifix of Santa Croce, the frescoes of the transept and the apse in Assisi, and the *Maestà* which was formerly in Santa Trinità and is now in the Uffizi Gallery. These were all painted before or just after 1280, and the experiments undertaken up to that time became fused in them in a clamorous religious fervour which alone might have inspired the art of a whole century. The barbaric accents of neo-Latin Italy which cry out in the work of Cimabue are still heard in the works of later artiste—Duccio and Giotto above all; as we see in the sublime *Madonna* of Castelfiorentino, in the *Maestà* in the Servi Church in Bologna, or in the *St John* of the apse mosaic in Pisa Cathedral, which the artist worked on in 1301-2, perhaps a few years before his death.

Plate 13—JACOPO TORRITI: Coronation (*Mosaic.*) In 1291 Jacopo Torriti, together with a fellow-monk, Friar Jacopo da Camerino, signed the apse mosaic of the basilica of St John Lateran, which owing to modern restorations, is now but a feeble copy of itself. Yet it is possible to see, from certain iconographic peculiarities, that the artist had modelled his work on an Early Christian prototype. This is significant in that it helps us to understand Torriti's later work in the great apse decoration of Santa Maria Maggiore, of about 1295. Pope Nicholas IV, perhaps because of his Franciscan past, chose the Franciscan Torriti for this undertaking. The artist's signature can be read on the left of the apse: JACOBUS TORRITI PICTOR HOC OPUS MOSIACUM FECIT.

In the centre of the apse, on a reduced scale, the same Pope is shown together with Cardinal Giacomo Colonna, who was to have the work continued after the death of Nicholas IV in 1292. The Coronation of the Virgin by Christ dominates the composition; this seems to derive from similar Roman representations of the 12th century; but it is not unlikely that the same theme appeared already in the mosaic of the original apse, in the time of Sixtus III. Christ and the Virgin are seated on the same throne, against a background of stars; their tunics and cloaks emphasise the modelling of the bodies, and the plastic quality of the forms is achieved by the distribution of light and shade. There seems no doubt, in fact, that Torriti had recourse to classical sources at least on this occasion, as Cavallini at the same time in Santa Maria in Trastevere was working in the same direction. Angels crowd close to the great aureole, while SS. Francis, Paul, Peter, John the Baptist, John the Evangelist and Anthony stand in contemplation. The end of the apse is decorated above these figures with acanthus patterns, whose blue-green branches reflect golden lights, and it is obvious that this theme was an echo of one dear to Early Christian art (as is shown by a comparison with the small, beautiful apse of the time of Sixtus III, in the atrium of St John Lateran).

But this does not exhaust the borrowings from late classical sources. The personification of the river pouring water from a pitcher is an obvious evocation of ancient art; so too are the little angels on the water, the boats, the fishermen and the animals in the picture. The scene in based on a literary text which was very well known in the Hellenistic age, the *Images* of Philostratus. Almost certainly Torriti merely renewed a theme which must already have existed in the original apse. To complete the apse decoration of Santa Maria Maggiore, floral friezes and figures of angels adorn the under-arch, and episodes from the life of the Virgin, the fillet below the vault (the *Annunciation*, the *Adoration of the Magi*, the *Presentation in the Temple*), with the *Dormitio Virginis* in the centre, which follows the iconograpny of Byzantine art derived from the Apocrypha. And there is not the slightest doubt that these scenes are

perfectly identical in style with the mosaic in the centre of the apse.

Plate 14—PIETRO CAVALLINI: Last Judgment. Detail of Christ the Judeg. (*Fresco*). Although Pietro Cavallini was highly considered at all times, we are not certain of the dates between which he worked, and critics are still divided as to how early or late his innovations were made, and as to the consequent importance of their influence on late 13th-century art. At that time, Italian painting passed through a period of evolution, due to the creative impulse of some great artists who were together responsible for the renaissance of the arts. It is, however, doubtful that Cavallini was a determining factor in that evolutionary process, as the earliest known date of one of his works is 1291 (inscribed below the apse mosaics of Santa Maria in Trastevere). Nor is this doubt dispelled by the slightly later and more evolved frescoes of Santa Cecilia, probably of the same date as Arnolfo's ciborium in that church—that is, 1293. These works, together with the fresco on the tomb of Cardinal Matteo d'Acquasparta, who died in 1302, are the only undisputed works of Cavallini, and it is on them that any serious study of his work must be based.

The mosaics of Santa Maria in Trastevere, which earned the praise of Ghiberti, show the greatest nobility of intellect. With penetrating intelligence, Cavallini selected and synthesised the art of early times and of his day. It is in fact difficult to separate this compendium of ancient and modern, incompletely fused in a new form of expression, from that which in contrast can be called true creation. Coming at the end of a very traditional period of art for Rome and southern Italy, Cavallini retained much of the rigid Oriental tradition, as can be seen in his iconographic archaism and in the technique of the fresco itself, where he employed the old encaustic method.

'He has something of the ancient, that is to say the Greek, manner,' observed Ghiberti; and it is true that an icon-like abstraction, a detachment, distinguish the cold and proud limbo of Cavallini from the fervour of the great contemporary Tuscan reformers, Arnolfo and Giotto especially, with their fresh and acute vision. From them Cavallini took the plastic definition of volumes and spatial relationships of composition, but reduced to a tender and delicate chromatic effect. He left behind for ever the coldness of abstract design, and of the Oriental colouristic tradition, and turned towards new ideals—without, however sharing in all the experimentation and newly discovered naturalism of his contemporaries.

In these mosaics, therefore, the green and plush meadows of early Christian mosaic art flower again with renewed vitality, and the Byzantine iconographic forms bend in the warmth of a gentle narrative.

In the frescoes of Santa Cecilia (discovered in the nuns' secret choir behind the entrance wall of the church, which had for many centuries hidden, and in great part hopelessly spoilt, the great *Last Judgment*) the gentle harmony of the timidly rounded forms—as timid as those of Giotto and Arnolfo had been bold in modelling and foreshortening—brings Cavallini's art close to the mysterious charm of Duccio, although without the historical rediscovery of an ancient ideal of beauty attained by his great contemporary.

Uncertain whether to follow Duccio or Giotto, Cavallini, in the fresco in Aracoeli for Cardinal Matteo d'Acquasparta, depicting the *Virgin between St John and St Francis, with Donor*, combined both styles in a work of great refinement and intellect but without the strength of inspiration of those great artists.

Plate 12. CIMABUE:
Crucifix. Arezzo, San Domenico.

Plate 13. JACOPO TORRITI:
Coronation. Mosaic. Rome, Santa Maria Maggiore.

Plate 14. PIETRO CAVALLINI:
Last Judgment. Detail of *Christ the Judge*.
Fresco. Rome, Santa Cecilia in Trastevere.

After the Neapolitan frescoes of 1308, believed to be by him, there is little trace of the difficult career of Pietro Cavallini, who, however, in Rome, was ' most learned among all other artists ' (Ghiberti).

Plate 15—DUCCIO: Madonna of the Franciscans. Duccio di Buoninsegna was born in Siena about 1260, if a document of 1278 entrusting a commission to *Duccio pictori* by the Siena Commune refers to that artist. Other references are made in documents of 1279 and 1280, so as to leave no doubt of their identification with the great artist. However, the first documented and dated work did not appear until 1285, when the Company of the Laudesi, of Santa Maria Novella in Florence, ordered a large panel '*de pulcerima pictura*', of the '*figura de beate Marie Virginis et eius omnipotentis Filii et aliarum figurarum*.' After this, Sienese documents continue to refer to Duccio from time to time, until the death of the painter in 1318. The most important of these documents are those of 1302 concerning a *Maestà*, now lost, painted for the Nine Governors of Siena, and those from 1308 to 1311 regarding the great ancon of a *Maestà* with scenes from the life of Christ on the back, which was to be placed on the high altar of Siena Cathedral.

Duccio's development in still a matter of controversy. Some connect his early work with the local style of Guido da Siena, or of painters like the Byzantine master of the Altarpiece of St John the Baptist, in the Siena Pinacoteca, from whom the young artist had taken eastern elements, although he was to surpass his models by far. Others, who have made a more aetailed study of Duccio's style, believe that he was taught by Cimabue and worked in the upper church at Assisi under his direction (see the *Crucifixion* in the nave, and an angel in the transept). This thesis, held by Longhi, places Duccio among the highest artists of his time and explains the emancipation of Sienese culture, in the wake of Duccio, from the mechanical stylisations of Orientalised painting which still weighed upon local art, either directly or through Guido.

Taking from Cimabue the impassioned sincerity of the Early Christian spirit of the West, Duccio proceeded with prodigious inspiration towards new abstractions of an elegant, yet always lively classicism. In his skies, brilliant colours dissolve in wide lakes enclosed by the winding hills of a line which quivers like that of French Gothic. The architecture seems weighed down by precious stones, yet rises with the upsurge of a Gothic tower. The pauses in the rhythm echo across the background, or swell sails and silken clothes in a slow-moving harmony. This interpretation applies too to the great Laudesi *Maestà* ancon, later in the Rucellai Chapel in Santa Maria Novella, documented as of 1285, which for long was believed, even by scholars of repute, to be the work of Cimabue. Yet Cimabue's gloomy melancholy finds no affinity here with the grace and tenderness of Duccio, who transmutes the solemnity of the Florentine into a classical purity and brilliance.

Not far removed in time from this first great work by Duccio are some masterpieces ascribed to him by modern critics: the *Madonna*, formerly at Crevole, in the Opera del Duomo Museum in Siena, the stained glass in the apse of Siena Cathedral, of 1287, and the Crucifix of the Castello Orsini at Bracciano; or the minute tempera painting of the *Madonna Enthroned*, *Adored by Three Franciscans*, in the Siena Pinacoteca, which, although little larger than a small illuminated page, has the immeasurable breadth of a splendid large work. In all the early works of Duccio, the fragile grace of northern Gothic combines with Eastern abstractions, whose splendid and impeccable techniques are humanised by him.

Plate 16—DUCCIO: Christ Appearing on Lake Tiberias. This detail of *Christ Appearing on Lake Tiberias* shows us the quality of Duccio's painting when he gave the best of himself, as in the *Maestà* for the altar of Siena Cathedral. The great ancon, besides the *Virgin Enthroned between Angels and Saints*, in front, consisted of a predella and wings, where the greatest space was occupied by twenty-six stories of Christ's Passion, from the *Entry into Jerusalem* to the *Journey to Emmaus*. *Christ Appearing on Lake Tiberias*, here reproduced, belongs to the back of the panel and was placed above the stories of the Passion. This wing lacks the two central panels, which were certainly larger and must have represented, on the two sides, the *Annunciation* or the *Coronation of the Virgin*, and the *Ascension*. Another two panels are missing in the back predella, and others are in various museums and collections, separated from the ancon which, after being neglected for many centuries, has been put together again, imperfectly restored, in the Opera del Duomo Museum in Siena.

Duccio worked on the *Maestà* between 9th October, 1308 and 9th June, 1311, on which day the great work, with its brilliant golds and splendid colours, was solemnly carried, among the festive people, from Duccio's studio to the Cathedral altar.

The event was told in these words by an unknown chronicler: 'And at that said time predicted by the Government the panel of the high altar was made and the one which today stands at the altar of San Boniface was removed, which is called the *Madonna of the Large Eyes* or the *Madonna of Grace*. Now it was this Madonna which granted the prayer of the people of Siena, when the Florentines were defeated at Monte Aperto; and so this painting was changed, because the new one was made which is much more beautiful and devout and greater, and has on the right side the Old and New Testament. And on that day when it was brought to the Cathedral, the shops were closed and the Bishop ordained a great and devout company of priests and friars in solemn ceremony, accompanied by the Nine Governors and all the Officials of the Commune and all the people, and all the most worthy went near to the said painting with lighted lamps in their hands; and then behind the women and children followed in great devotion; and they accompanied the said painting right to the Cathedral, taking up position around the campo as is usual, and all the bells ringing to glory and devotion for such a noble painting as this. Which painting was made by Duccio di Niccolò, painter, in the house of the Muciatti outside the gate at Stallorreggi. And all that day was passed in prayer and good works.'

This moving record enables us to understand just what Duccio's masterpiece represented to the people of Siena. It expressed the prestige of a now tempered tradition, and the heartfelt devotion which sustained it could have no more precious monument. That tradition was all contained in the genius of Duccio, who had inaugurated it thirty years previously; and while in the meantime he had not ceased to grow in depth, yet he never broke away from his original direction, of the *Rucellai Madonna* or the panel of the *Franciscans*. Not even the example of Giotto's tremendous achievement could modify or in any way change Duccio's style; and even less so could Giovanni Pisano, who was in Siena during the last decade of the 13th century.

Unfortunately only a few works remain of that period, among them the *Madonna,* No. 583 in the Siena Pinacoteca, the *Madonna* in

Plate 16. DUCCIO:
Christ Appearing on Lake Tiberias. Siena, Opera del Duomo Museum.

Plate 15. DUCCIO:
Madonna of the Franciscans. Siena, Pinacoteca.

the Stoclet Collection in Brussels, the *Madonna* in the Perugia Gallery, and the triptych in the National Gallery in London. In all these works, ancient rhythms gently unfold with melancholy grace to portray the devotion and pathos of an ideal of humanity which was an endlessly sought-after symbol of a concept not of this earth.

Plate 17—GIOTTO: The Renunciation of Wordly Goods (*Detail*). In 1296 Giovanni di Muro, of the Franciscan Order, commissioned Giotto, according to Vasari, to paint the frescoes of the story of St Francis in the nave of the upper church of the basilica of St Francis at Assisi. Giotto had already been working in the basilica for many years, alongside other pupils of Cimabue and some groups of less skilled artists from southern Italy. During that period, between 1285 and 1290, and also around 1295, Giotto had been painting in the upper part of the same nave many Old and New Testament stories in which the young Florentine applied brilliantly the lessons of Cimabue—but expressed in a new way which owed much to the experiments in volume of Arnolfo di Cambio. Looking at some of these early frescoes, the *Lamentation over the Dead Christ*, *Pentecost* and the *Marys at the Tomb*, we see a world of paint forming into planes and relations of volume—with a breathing and corporate humanity being created, which was suffering and living in the physical reality of the event enacted. The world once more became populated and clothed in colour, but the moral contrition of Cimabue was no longer present.

In the story of St Francis, because of the modern content, which was almost that of a contemporary chronicle, Giotto no longer needed to borrow from the art of the past. Art could be conceived in everyday terms, and this was to remain fundamental to each successive evolution of painting in Italy. With Giotto, distances take on a full and living significance of physical spaciousness, and volumes confirm their own substance in terms of plastic energy. In the *Gift of the Cloak to the Poor Knight*, we see Giotto's cubistic treatment of the landscape and the figures, and we admire at the same time the Umbrian landscape and the humanity of the characters who find in it the space and authentic conditions for revealing themselves in the touching piety of their acts. These acts already belong to the realm of gentle legend, yet they are of striking, evident truth. This has been brought about by Giotto, for the *Miracle of St Francis Preaching to the Birds* and the *Miracle of the Thirsty Man* seem born of his imagination rather than to illustrate the beliefs of the followers of St Francis of Assisi.

The Franciscan cycle is related in twenty-eight frescoes, three to each bay and two on the wall in the entrance to the church. But not all the scenes were painted by Giotto. He worked alone on almost the whole of the first wall (to the right facing the altar) and of the entrance wall, whereas the intervention of collaborators is very obvious on the left wall, where the artistic merit is much less. Yet even this last part of the decoration is not without exquisite passages by the hand of Giotto, for example: the *Stigmata of St Francis*, almost the whole of the *Appearance to the Chapter of Arles*, and the beautiful *Appearance to Gregory IX*. The last three scenes, by an admirable unknown painter, probably a Florentine, are different in style; this painter was one of many who grew up under the influence of Giotto, which was still of the 13th century.

It is reasonably maintained that the whole decoration was completed during the Jubilee Year of 1300. The recourse to numerous assistants in the final episodes can be explained by the urgency of completing the task in time.

Plate 17. GIOTTO:
The Renunciation of Wordly Goods. Detail. Assisi, Church of St Francis, Upper Church.

Three of these episodes: the *Dream of Innocent III*, the *Confirmation of the Order* and *St Francis Preaching to the Birds*, recur soon after in the predella of the *Stigmata* (which is now in the Louvre and was formerly in the church of St Francis in Pisa), signed *Opus Jocti florentini*. From this we have plain proof that the whole Assisi cycle is ascribable to Giotto, a fact which some critics have persistently laid open to doubt.

Plate 18—GIOTTO: The Meeting of Joachim and Anna. (*Detail*). Giotto began work on the frescoes of the Arena Chapel in Padua after the 25th March, 1303, when Enrico Scrovegni founded the little church, dedicated to the Virgin of the Annunciation. Two years later, on 25th March, 1305, the chapel was consecrated and Venice was asked to send cloth for the vestments. On the same date the following year, the Feast of the Madonna of the Arena was instituted. These dates enable scholars to fix the periods of Giotto's work on the frescoes. It must have taken him more than a year to complete such a huge undertaking. The frescoes follow the Franciscan frescoes in Assisi and precede what remains of his work in Rimini, before 1312-13 (the Crucifix of the Malatesta Temple), and within the cycle there is little evolution of style.

The *Stigmata of St Francis* in the Louvre, previously mentioned, and the polyptych depicting the *Madonna and Saints*, formerly in the Badia of Florence and now in the Santa Croce Museum, form a bridge between the Assisi and the Paduan periods, while the Crucifix of the Malatesta Temple, the *Dormitio Virginis* in the Berlin Museum, and finally the frescoes of the Peruzzi Chapel in Santa Croce, indicate the successive stages of Giotto's art.

A new monumental dimension is given in the Badia polyptych, but there must certainly have been other works by Giotto in the years between the work at Assisi and at Padua, which would explain the hiatus in style in this short period of less than five years.

Giotto's intellectual preparation in Florence in the early years of the century found magnificent fulfilment in the Scrovegni Chapel. The figures have a massive weight, a monumental equilibrium, and stand motionless and solemn in the clear light of the primary colours.

In the popular freshness of the Franciscan legend, Giotto showed the power of the religious feeling of the people by means of narration, yet within an organised stylistic scheme. In the scenes from the life of the Virgin and the episodes in the life of Christ he adapts to his own measure the morality of the true evangelist. In rapt solemnity, the gestures are fixed in an eternal pose, where time itself stands still.

In the Paduan frescoes Giotto rejects both the organic vitality of Romanesque art and the animated restless elegance of Gothic art. Their spaces and volumes reveal a magnificent coloured Bible, seen not from a supernatural viewpoint but through the inverted glass of memory.

Besides the scenes from the life of the Virgin in the highest fillet of the frescoes and the episodes in the life of Christ in the two lower registers, the Arena Chapel has the enormous *Last Judgment* fresco on the entrance wall, a vault decorated with stars and with medallions of Christ and the Virgin, each surrounded by four medallions containing portraits of the prophets, and a socle at the base of the walls containing allegories of the Vices and Virtues, painted in monochrome; while above the two paintings on the triumphal arch of the Angel of the Annunciation and Mary, is the *Eternal Entrusting His Message to the Archangel Gabriel*. And we should not overlook the two false funeral chapels, painted with perfect perspective, an imaginative *trompe l'oeil*, at the sides of the arch.

Plate 19—GIOTTO: Maestà. One of Giotto's most famous panels is the great *Maestà*, which he painted for the Florentine church of Ognissanti, together with some other paintings (*Dormitio Virginis*, in the Berlin Museum), and which is now in the Uffizi Gallery.

This panel was frequently mentioned as being by Giotto in early sources from Ghiberti onwards. It was recorded in a document in the Ognissanti church in 1418, and is accepted by modern critics as a fully authenticated work of Giotto. As for its probable date of completion, some critics (Thode, Toesca, etc.) believe it to precede the Scrovegni frescoes, while others (A. Venturi, Rintelen, Weigelt, Offner, Brandi, Gnudi) place it later. While inclining to the second opinion, that it followed the Paduan frescoes, we cannot exclude the possibility that the panel was executed during one of the winters which forced the artist to suspend work on the frescoes. The style of the panel seems closest to the earliest of the Paduan frescoes, the stories of Joachim and of the Virgin, while the later series of the episodes in the life of Christ, or the *Last Judgment*, most closely resemble the Crucifix, of the church of San Felice, which Venturi believed to be entirely the work of Giotto, and which can still be seen in Florence. Painted therefore about 1305, the Ognissanti *Maestà* expresses the same poetic ideals as the frescoes in Padua and provided a model for the innumerable Maestà altar-pieces of Tuscany in the 13th and 14th centuries, when it was endlessly imitated.

Giotto expressed the spiritual values of the sacrament in the same stylistic rigour admired in the Paduan frescoes. In the plastic concept of form, nothing appears of the Gothic unrest which then animated the whole of European art; but Giotto planned a highly calculated spatial relationship of volumes such as Arnolfo, the Florentine architect and sculptor, had employed.

The throne of Giotto's *Maestà* is architecturally constructed as a real support, while the decoration no longer resembles that of Cosma, as in the painted architecture of Assisi, but serves to integrate the creative elements of the new style which will be the basis of the architectonic tradition of Florence up to Brunelleschi. Without the throne, the breadth and gravity of the monumental *Madonna and Child* would not be so fully realised; it is placed for ever—an architecture within an architecture, in the shade of the small vault between foreshortened Gothic arches and the steps which cause the figures to recede, creating more space, as one mounts them. There remains space for the two kneeling angels in the foreground and for the angels and saints placed at the sides of the throne, they, too, mathematically scaled to converge.

We all know that these static forms, this rediscovered classical composure, were to stabilise the style prevalent in all Italian art in its search for 'divine proportions' and the clarity of the norm to which it always aspired.

After this great apogee of this art, Giotto's work developed further for many years, modulating in varied ways the forms already achieved, suggesting new solutions and new themes which for two generations inspired his followers in their own experiments. So the ornate tenderness of the Peruzzi Chapel was the model for the chromatic classicism of the great Stefano, the most important of Giotto's followers; so too the measured and monumental Cappella Bardi, also in Santa Croce, determined the mental direction of Maso di Bianco. Similarly, an earlier influence—the Ognissanti

Plate 18. GIOTTO:
The Meeting of Joachim and Anna. Detail. Padua, Arena Chapel.

style—had directed the steps of the more modest Taddeo Gaddi.

Plate 20—SIMONE MARTINI: Madonna and Child. Simone Martini began to paint just at the end of Duccio's career. In 1315, Simone painted for the rulers of Siena the great *Maestà* fresco in the Sala del Mappamondo in the Palazzo Pubblico. This was a revelation of formal elegance, inspired by a vision of the world as a luxurious and profane lie, to which he gave the pageantry of a Gothic dress which until then had seemed the preserve of northern art. From the very first, at least as far as we can affirm from present knowledge, Simone's painting owed a great deal to French Gothic. This is confirmed by documents recording the presence of the Sienese artist at the Neapolitan court of Robert d'Anjou, where in 1317 he executed the elegant ancon depicting *King Robert Crowned by St Louis of Toulouse*, now in the Capodimonte Museum, Naples. Here the slow-moving, compact rhythms of the *Maestà* in the Palazzo Pubblico unfold with gentle indolence, to depict a heraldic figure of fantastic abstraction. But within the painting there is a vitality, contrite and refined, melancholy and precious. In Naples the artist's direction was determined, and he always inclined towards the art of France from then on; indeed, he passed the last years of his life in that country.

After the return of the court of Anjou, a period of intense activity followed for Simone Martini. We can see numerous polyptychs in Pisa and Orvieto which are very much akin in style and which combine the ornate quality of the profane art practised in Naples with the mystic and ritualistic elements more appropriate to the severe liturgy and piety of the Umbrian and Tuscan churches.

The *Madonna and Child* found in Lucignano d'Arbia by Carli, now in the Siena Pinacoteca, dates from this time, that is, about 1320. Beneath a heavy overpainting, the pearl-like purity of the forms and colours of Simone has reappeared, complete in all the parts which have not been irreparably damaged by barbarous treatment. The gold ground and the blue lapis lazuli of the Virgin's cloak are entirely lost. But in the painting which has survived are the whole of the Madonna's face and the body of the Child. The bowed, sad face of the Virgin is in every way a sister to those faces in the centre of the polyptychs of Santa Caterina at Pisa (1319) and the one in the Cathedral Museum of Orvieto, or again in the triptych, formerly in Orvieto, which is now in the Gardner Museum in Boston.

It was probably after this time, in the third decade of the century, that Simone worked on the fresco of the life of St Martin in the chapel of the lower church of the basilica of St Francis at Assisi. It is perhaps from this cycle of frescoes that the Sienese artist has the greatest claim to glory. With inexpressible originality he brought to that church, which had formerly been entirely given over to the art of Florence, a style founded largely, as we have seen, upon French elements which were quite strange to Florentine art, and he laid the foundations of a new Franco-Italian figurative style. These frescoes are among the most rare and influential achievements which the Italian 14th century can boast; and to them the courtly painters were to turn once more.

Plate 21—SIMONE MARTINI: Annunciation. In 1333, Simone Martini, together with Lippo Memmo, signed the triptych of the *Annunciation* (centre), with *St Ansanus* and *Santa Giustina* on the side panels. The frame

Plate 19. GIOTTO:
Maestà. Florence, Uffizi Gallery.

is modern, and was placed on the panels in the last century when they were removed to the Uffizi Gallery from the church of San Ansano in Siena, where they had been since the 18th century although originally painted for the Cathedral. When the frame was applied, the original fillet was saved and encased in the new surround. On this fillet is the inscription: SIMON . MARTINI . ET . LIPPVS . MEMMI . DE . SENIS . ME . PINXERVNT . ANNO . DOMINI . MCCCXXXIII . Scholars are now agreed on the origins of the parts. Simone's hand is seen in the central *Annunciation*, as Berenson first suggested, and that of Lippo Memmi, his brother-in-law, in the painting of the two saints, who were, however, painted over a sketch by Simone.

The *Annunciation*, thus established as the work of Simone Martini, is like an elegant cipher which embellishes in balanced rhythm the vast golden field. It was to remain an unforgettable and fascinating model for successive generations of Sienese painters, and was copied as late as the 15th century by Domenico di Bartolo. Simone appears to emulate the precious art of the miniaturist, yet without renouncing the grandeur of concept of the Sienese tradition. The freshness of his inspiration and his inimitable genius in this work found no comparison in his later style, although he produced works just as great.

A glance at the paintings which precede and follow the Uffizi *Annunciation* confirms this. In 1328, Simone had planned for the Sala del Mappamondo in the Palazzo Pubblico the great frieze to the Sienese leader Guidoriccio da Fogliano. The republic celebrates the victory of Castruccio Castracani in the battle of Montemassi and Sassoforte. The victorious captain rides his steed, which gently prances in the centre of a landscape of grey clay, among tiny palings with their echoes of lances and standards. On dwarf-like hills, Sassoforte and Montemassi stand out sharply as if engraved against the blue background. So the imagination of 14th-century artists was to wander in the fields of fantasy.

Not even after 1333, the year of the *Annunciation*, was Simone Martini to change to a less fabulous and unreal form of art. There are few works which we are certain belong to the time just before his death, in Avignon in 1344. Of these, only the *Childhood of Jesus*, in the Liverpool Gallery, and the miniature of the frontispiece of Petrarch's *Virgil*, now in the Milan Gallery, which was painted by Simone for his friend Petrarch certainly after 1340, when the poet found the codex he had lost in 1328, are definitely works of this time. Petrarch himself noted in these two Latin verses that the miniature was the work of Martini:

> Mantua Virgilium, qui talia carmina fluxit
> Sena tulit Symonem, digito qui talia pinxit.

And it was this page more than any other work, with its meadows and laurels, that had the greatest influence on the direction which was to be taken by the supreme follower of Martini, the Avignonese artist Matteo Giovanetti da Viterbo, the last, perhaps, of the great 14th-century artists.

The *Childhood of Jesus* in the Walker Art Gallery, Liverpool, is dated 1342. It is part of a diptych separated in the last century, and is a work of great originality. It breaks away from the 14th-century forms usually employed to represent a static image or sacred episode, and instead the dialogue and the action are in continual movement, within a decoration ornate as that of a luxurious profane ceremony.

Plate 22—PIETRO LORENZETTI: Madonna and Child. (*Detail of polyptych*). On the 17th April, 1320, Bishop Guido Tarlati

commissioned Pietro Lorenzetti to paint the polyptych for the high altar of the Pieve Church in Arezzo. This is fortunately still in its original place and is almost entirely intact. The signature reads: PETRVX . LAVRENTII . HANC . PINXIT . DEXTRA . SENENSIS . On either side of the Virgin are SS. Donatus, John the Evangelist, John the Baptist and Matthew; in the upper register, on a reduced scale, are eight saints with the Annunciation in the centre; in the wings are four saints and the Virgin of the Assumption.

The document granting the commission of this work gives 1320 as the earliest date of execution, and this remains the first known work which can be ascribed with certainty to Pietro Lorenzetti. At that time he could not have been very young, if a Sienese document of 1306 which mentions 'Petruccio di Lorenzo' refers to him, and if a group of works referred to by critics as the first decade of his activity are in fact the work of Lorenzetti. Of these early works, the best known are: the *Madonna of Monticchlello*, on either side of which were the *Three Saints*, now in the Horne Museum, Florence, and *Saint Margaret*, now in Le Mans; the *Madonna Enthroned* in the Diocesan Museum of Cortona; the Crucifix in the same museum. In all these panels a powerful personality emerges, who moves from the school of Duccio in Siena of 1310 towards artists with whom he feels greater affinity—Giovanni Pisano and Giotto. It was before Giotto's work in Assisi, soon after 1310, that Pietro felt his tie with that artist, and in his work he tempered the harsh truth of Giotto's plastic art with echoes of the golden rhythms of Duccio. But the young Sienese artist was influenced by the sculpture of Giovanni Pisano and his contemporary Tino da Camaino, with its charged expressiveness forced into a disciplined form.

After the fresco painting of a triptych of the *Virgin between St John Baptist and St Francis*, in the Orsini Chapel, in the left transept of the basilica of St Francis at Assisi, Pietro painted in the same transept of the lower church the six scenes from Christ's Passion. An enamelled surface of colour glows in these frescoes on the vault, in the brilliant tradition of Siena, but in form they are tormented by a sorrowful anguish.

It is at this point that we have the equivalent of Pietro's style in the *Pieve Polyptych* in Arezzo, the central image of which, the *Madonna and Child*, leaves no doubt of the artist's wish to emulate in pictorial form the sculpture of Giovanni Pisano The figures of the Mother and her Child are painted with great emotional intensity; the powerful masses seem to writhe as if to forge a small space for themselves in their golden niche, and the outlines of the figures have a mournful grace.

After 1320, Pietro Lorenzetti painted the splendid *Crucifixion* in the same transept of St Francis' in Assisi, and below the *Crucifixion*, the famous *Virgin between St Francis and St John the Evangelist*. In this work, the theme of the conversation breaks through the limits of the triptical partition, and presents an iconographic formula of genius, very premature for its time. And equally amazing is the elegant crowd of sorrowful, curious or pathetic bystanders, who crowd the Hill of Calvary at the foot of the three crosses.

The great altar-piece depicting the *Madonna Enthroned, with Saints*, which was formerly in the Carmine church and is now in the Siena Pinacoteca, dates from 1329. In this and in other works Pietro measured his genius with the growing Florentine culture of the period after Giotto's time. He continued to do so for the whole of his life, even after he settled in his native Siena. The proportions of the masses and the taste for colour, of no less vigour than before, now take on a calculated and solemn measure, which must have owed something to the example of the Florentine,

Plate 20. SIMONE MARTINI:
Madonna and Child. Lucignano d'Arbia, Parish church.

Plate 21. SIMONE MARTINI:
Annunciation. Uffizi Gallery, Florence.

Plate 22. PIETRO LORENZETTI:
Madonna and Child. Detail of polyptych. Arezzo, Pieve Church.

Maso di Banco. The same might be said of the *Madonna* in the Loeser Collection or the small ancon in the Poldi Pezzoli Museum in Milan, the triptych in the Dijon Museum, the altar-piece in the Walters Museum, Baltimore, and even the solemn *Madonna Enthroned, with Angels*, dated 1340, in the Uffizi Gallery, or the polyptych, also in the Uffizi, of the *Beatitude*, which was painted before the *Birth of the Virgin*, with its amazing spatial invention, now in the Opera del Duomo Museum in Siena, and dated 1342.

Plate 23—AMBROGIO LORENZETTI: Allegory of Good and Bad Government. (*Frescoes*). No less than his brother Pietro, Ambrogio Lorenzetti showed from his first known work an obvious connection with the art of Florence—of Giotto especially. That first work is the *Madonna Enthroned*, in the church of Sant'Angiolo at Vico l'Abate, dated: A.D. MCCCXVIIII; it may even have been painted in Florence, where Ambrogio lived for long periods of time and was inscribed in the register of the Medici and Speziali. There is no need to stress the Florentine architectonic conception of form as shown in the static and massive conception of that superb painting, with its lively drawing expressing the tension of the modelling.

This stylistic union between Florence and Siena, which can already be seen in the icon of Vico l'Abate, becomes more obvious still in the two frescoes in the church of St Francis in Siena, depicting the *Martyrdom of the Franciscans at Ceuta* and *St Louis of Toulouse received by Boniface VIII*. In these lively frescoes, and in others in the same church which are now lost, the earliest writers, from Ghiberti onwards, found much to admire. Already, to the writers of the 15th century, Ambrogio seemed a painter of miraculous and unrestrained fantasy, of caustic sharpness, of amazing wisdom and erudition. He was famed, too, as a refined humanist of great subtlety of mind, and even as an archaeologist, if it was really he who classified the statue of Venus which was dug up in Sienese territory, only to be hastily reburied by the scandalised citizens of the enemy territory of Florence. This episode is a significant illustration of the experimental spirit of the Italian 14th century, which was not yet able to assimilate models which contaminated the living source of moral reality or of the developing art.

Ambrogio Lorenzetti enriched the art of Siena, not only in form, but, more significantly, in emotion, in his tender humanity. His work stands apart from the generally more mysterious and detached Tuscan art. His numerous portrayals of the Madonna and Child which in their flowing lines take on a humanity, an almost 'tense languor', henceforth belong to a universal patrimony. His paintings emulate the splendour of the most ornate icons, yet with great pungency and subtlety of form. One of the most significant of Ambrogio's paintings is the great *Maestà* in the Town Hall of Massa Marittima. The crowds of saints about the steps of the throne, in spite of the repetition in the composition, produce a smiling sensation which will give pleasure to Sassetta almost a hundred years later, when in a similar way he will combine naturalistic truth with stylistic abstraction.

In the richness of his themes we can see the worldly and polite vision he tirelessly revealed for the edification of all kinds of visual curiosity—like the *Globe* which, as we know from early sources, he painted for the fantasy of Sienese science.

So the *Allegories of Good and Bad Government*, in the Hall of Peace in the Siena Palazzo Pubblico, which were painted from 1337 to 1339, contain the whole sharpness of description which the Gothic painting of Tuscany was able to express. A lively panorama of the city shows streets and squares crowded with citizens going about their work or pleasures; and the observer who lingers there, stopping between the cobbler's shop and the grammar school, will always take some fresh item of news to add to the ' Chronicle of Siena ' of that most fortunate time. Lively, too, is the view of the countryside, like an enormous flowered map illustrating the peaceful days in the calendar of the peasant and the hunter. On the next wall, which portrays the good government of the republic, the citizens file past, in fine pomp, somewhat grave and somewhat festive, in honour of the symbol of their communal liberty; after the remoteness of the art of the past, this fresco foreshadows the very direct and human bourgeois painting which was to follow.

As in the case of his brother Pietro, the year of the birth and death of Ambrogio are not known, although we know that he died after 1347; while the last date on one of his works is inscribed on the *Annunciation* in the Siena Pinacoteca as the year 1344.

Plate 24—GIOVANNI DA MILANO: Joachim Thrust from the Temple. (*Fresco*). The earliest mention we have of Giovanni di Giacomo di Guido da Como, or, as he signed himself, ' da Milano ', is in a Florentine document of 1346 which dealt only with foreign painters residing in Florence. Yet no work of this artist remains which can be certified as of an earlier date than 1360, and then only in Prato and Florence, and none which can be dated with absolute certainty as earlier than 1365, in which year a document refers to the frescoes of Santa Croce; and Giovanni painted a *Pietà* on panel, now in the Accademia Gallery in Florence, which is signed: IO GIOVANNI DE MELANO DEPINSI QUESTA TAVOLA I MCCCLXV. Giovanni is mentioned also in documents concerning his being granted Florentine citizenship in 1366; and his presence in the Vatican in 1369, together with Giovanni and Agnolo Gaddi and Giottino di Maestro Stefano, is mentioned for the task of painting two chapels for Urbano V.

Although these documents were all Florentine or Roman, Giovanni's origins were decidedly Lombard. But painting in Lombardy before 1346 was not sufficiently developed to explain the art of Giovanni, which has therefore been considered as being closely allied to that of the Florentine, or, at any rate, Tuscan painters, who, to escape the plague, left Florence in 1348, and then worked with the fresco painters of the Umiliati Abbey in Viboldone, near Milan, which was consecrated in the very same year, 1348. This would explain the great affinity between Giovanni's art and that of Giusto de' Menabuoni, who was among these refugees, and also that of Giottino, whose work can be seen in the wonderful fresco formerly in the campanile of San Gottardo in Milan. The second half of the century saw numerous Lombard frescoes which were obviously influenced by Giovanni's mature style; for he must have returned to his home after his first stay in Florence and left there traces of his work in some fresco cycles which are now lost.

This hypothesis by Roberto Longhi solves the problem of Giovanni's early formation, which could neither be explained by references to Lombard painting of the first half of the century, from Vitale da Bologna to Tomaso da Modena, nor by taking the view that Giovanni lived in Tuscany from 1346 without interruption. Such an uninterrupted stay could but have diminished the strong Lombard and continental influences which, however, are very noticeable in the work of this artist. Moreover, no Florentine works of his exist which are earlier in style than the seventh decade of

PAX

Plate 24. GIOVANNI DA MILANO
Joachim Thrust from the Temple. Fresco. Florence, Santa Croce.

Plate 23. AMBROGIO LORENZETTI:
Allegory of Good Government. Detail of fresco. Siena, Palazzo Pubblico.

the century. The Lombard spirit can be seen in his naturalism and in the play of light and shade over the surface of every object, which is held together in the lucid vitality of the shadowy distances. A new intensity of vision foreshadows the microcosmic images of the last of the Gothic painters of Lombardy and Burgundy, and of the van Eycks themselves.

With Giovanni da Milano the union of the glorious plastic style of Tuscany with the naturalism of the north is foreshadowed, which would mix dream and reality for the refined and profane taste of courts, until the decline of European Gothic art.

But that polite and courtly art has not yet appeared in the work of Giovanni da Milano, whose grave and serious attitude is highly religious in character. The polyptych in the Prato Museum, in which naturalism and devotion are interwoven, is perhaps the earliest of a series of works which are very closely related and which includes the panel in the Rome National Gallery, the *Crucifixion*, formerly in the Seymour-Maynard collection, the triptych in London and *Christ in Judgment* in the Contini-Bonacossi Collection in Florence, painted at the same time as the *Pietà* in the Accademia and the Rinuccini frescoes, in 1365. Slightly later in date are the dismembered polyptych in the Uffizi, the eleven saints in the Sabauda Gallery in Turin, the sublime *Pietà* in the Le Roy Collection, the predellas in the Bacri Collection, the *St Francis*, formerly in the Bordeaux Museum, and the lunette in the Metropolitan Museum.

The frescoes in the Rinuccini Chapel in the sacristy of Santa Croce contain episodes in the lives of Joachim, Christ and the Magdalen, with the exception of the lower register, which is by a mediocre Florentine painter, a follower of Orcagna. In the centre of the vault is the tempera painting on panel of the *Benediction of Christ*.